Jean Jacques
Bourasse

, Andrew Lang

The miracles of Madame Saint Katherine of Fierbois

Jean Jacques
Bourasse

, Andrew Lang

The miracles of Madame Saint Katherine of Fierbois

ISBN/EAN: 9783743364905

Manufactured in Europe, USA, Canada, Australia, Japa

Cover: Foto ©ninafisch / pixelio.de

Manufactured and distributed by brebook publishing software (www.brebook.com)

Jean Jacques
Bourasse

, Andrew Lang

The miracles of Madame Saint Katherine of Fierbois

The miracles of madame saint Katherine of Fierbois

translated from the editi͠n of the abbé J. J. Bourassé, Tours, 1858: by Andrew Lang

Chicago: Way and Williams
London: David Nutt.
1897

THE DE VINNE PRESS, NEW YORK, U. S. A.

The title-page, the head- and tail-pieces, and the initials in this book are the work of Selwyn Image.

PREFACE

Invited by my friend Mr. Way to translate a little book as a companion to my version of "Aucassin and Nicolete," I could find nothing more curious than the Abbé Bourassé's edition of the Fierbois Chapel chronicle, "Les Miracles de Madame Sainte Katherine" (Manuscript in the Bibliothèque Nationale). One or two very dull narratives I have ventured to omit, and have added an essay on Fierbois and the Maid's connection with the shrine.

INTRODUCTION

E read in history for various reasons and to various ends. Now we are allured by the tale of human adventure in the world, and the drama of the fortunes of nations; again we are attracted by some personality, as of Napoleon, or Cortés, or Mary Stuart; or we try to interpret the present and the future by the past, and to learn the lesson which peoples, like individuals, can only be taught by actual experience, and then too late.

But history has another charm, and the historic muse might be represented gazing in the mystic glass which reflects all the changing aspects of common life that is no more, and the days that do not return. No gift would be more enviable than the visionary power of seeing the departed generations in their costumes as they lived, concerned with the many trivial accidents that were things of habit to them, and that now have passed wholly out of the existence which we know.

Shreds of old raiment, ancient coffers, armor, swords, jewels, we can look at in the museums; but fancy fails when she tries to restore the pictures of the men and women to whom these were things of quotidian use and service. The traits, minute but essential, of the lost time escape us; to live an hour in old Athens or in medieval Paris would teach us far more than we can gain from chronicle, or from art. Nevertheless the love of the spectacle of life makes us treasure every hint from book or manuscript concerning details of existence which are rarely mentioned by writers to whom they seemed over familiar and over trivial for record. We hear of princes and captains in the great wars, but we are seldom informed about the hinds who were plundered, and the common archers and men-at-arms who were food for the appetite of the sword.   In search of lore which will complete our knowledge, and fill our picture of the past, we turn from the great chronicles, as now from those of Monstrelet, Chastelain, or Froissart, into such byways of the past as the little old French manuscript which is here translated for the first time.*

The official contemporary record of *Les Miracles de Madame Sainte Katherine de Fierboys* seems to bring us almost within sight and touch of France during the late middle ages, and in the agony of the Hundred Years' War with England.   When Jeanne d'Arc, in the most hopeless

* From the edition by the Abbé J. J. Bourassé. Mame & Cie., Tours, 1858.

hour of France (February, 1429), rode
from Vaucouleurs to lead the dis-
tracted armies of the Dauphin, she
paused at Fierbois, a little town within a day's ride of Chinon, and there,
in the Church of Saint Katherine, she
heard three masses. Around her, on
the walls, hung the votive offer-
ings, not only of sick folk whom
"the glorious virgin, Madame Saint
Katherine," had healed, but of bur-
gesses, laborers, knights, and squires,
French or Scots, whom she had miraculously released from English dun-
geons and from death at English
hands. Fierbois is distant from the
parts of France, such as Normandy,
Picardy, and Aquitaine, which England had recently conquered or held

by long traditional right. Nevertheless, out of many a remote province,
by many a perilous way, men had
made pilgrimage, since the year 1375,
to praise Madame Saint Katherine
for death miraculously avoided, or for
dungeon-doors that opened of their
own accord (as to Saint Peter in
prison), or for irons that fell marvel-
ously from the limbs of the devout.
At Fierbois pilgrims consecrated the
chains which failed to bind them,
the rope that did not hang them,
the arrow that dropped innocuous
out of the wound, or the culverin
ball that slipped harmless from the
body. The spectacle of these relics
was reinforced by the chapel record,
containing the confessions of the men

whom beyond all hope Saint Katherine had delivered. Doubtless these stories were recited to Jeanne d'Arc, the peasant girl who "did not know A from B," and all that she saw and heard at Fierbois must have strengthened the faith of La Pucelle in the saint who, with Saint Margaret and Saint Michael, was her own familiar friend.

A month later, when Jeanne was accepted by the voice of the clergy of her party, when the Dauphin was presenting her with horses, weapons, rich robes, and shining armor, she remembered the chapel of Saint Katherine of Fierbois. From Charles she would take no sword; her "voices" bade her bear an ancient weapon, with five crosses on the blade, which was to be found under the earth behind the altar of Saint Katherine. An armorer was sent from Tours to make search, and the sword was discovered in the place indicated by the "voices." Shakspere, or whoever wrote the deplorable First Part of Henry VI, mocks at this discovery, which had a great effect in rousing popular enthusiasm. The early history of the sword of Fierbois, and its later fate are alike unknown. The Maid broke it when beating a leaguer-lass with the flat of the blade, soon after her victory at Patay, and the King's armorers could not repair the weapon. It was thought that now her

16

good fortune left her; but the dauntless Maid captured a sword from a Burgundian, "a good cut and thrust piece," as she described it. At her trial, she declined to tell her judges where she had bestowed the sacred weapon. The tradition which calls the Fierbois sword that of Charles Martel (who defeated the paynim at Tours), I have not succeeded in tracing further back than Chapelain's epic of *La Pucelle*, published in 1656.

Here the connection of Jeanne d'Arc with Fierbois ends, though in the chapel record we learn that on May 5, 1430, Jean Boucher said a mass for "the King, and the Maid, the worthy servant of God." Eighteen days later, the Maid was taken by a Picard in a sally from Compiégne. Not for this illustrious captive did Saint Katherine work any of the miracles whereof she was so profuse.·

It was one of the charges against Jeanne that she constantly gazed at a little ring of base metal, the gift of her parents, which bore the sacred names, *Jhesus, Marie.* One who had seen her thus gazing mentioned the practice to Bower, the continuator of the Scottish Chronicle of Fordun. She herself, at her trial, explained that she loved the ring because therewith, as she believed, she had touched the body of Saint Katherine. She asserted that she had often embraced her saints, but it is possible that, as the custom was, she had touched with her ring the relics of the body of Saint Katherine, which are still preserved at Fierbois. She refused, it may be noted, to say what portion of the saint's body the ring had touched.   Now at Mount Sinai the relics of the saint, whose body was borne thither by angels, are kept, and silver rings which have been in contact with them are still presented to pilgrims by the religious; it seems probable, therefore, as Father Ayroles remarks, that the Fierbois relics were brought thither by a French Crusader who acquired them at Mount Sinai.   Fierbois became a center of the cult of Saint Katherine, but by 1375, through the ruin of war, her chapel had fallen into utter disuse, and was overgrown by the wildwood. In that year, as we learn from the chapel register, one Jehan Godefroy, of Fierbois, was completely paralyzed, and was also blind. He remembered, after seven years of suffering, that there had been an old chapel of Madame Saint Katherine in a certain place. Thither he was carried, as if through the enchanted wood of the Sleeping Beauty, "*lequel estoit plain de grans boys, de buissons et ronces, et si n'estoit nul quy y peust avenir.*" "Through tangled wood and undergrowth no man might reach the deserted chapel," yet there Jehan Godefroy determined to make his *neuvaine*. His men, therefore, hewed with axes a path through the forest; Godefroy was laid within the desecrated walls, and before his *neuvaine* was ended "he could see well and clear, and was whole and healed in all his members, as he yet continues to be." The chapel was consequently rebuilt in the same year by Hylaire Habert, to the indignation of his wife, as we read in the first miracle of the present collection.

When we ask for facts about the "thaumaturgic agency" about the wonder-working Saint connected with Fierbois by popular belief, the answer is vague; indeed, practically we get no answer at all. Who was

Saint Katherine of Alexandria, the patron of the chapel in Touraine? A chaplain of Saint Katherine's Hall in Cambridge, Mr. Charles Hardwick, has written an essay on the subject, and has left it unproved that Saint Katharine of Alexandria was a real person.   Her name is naturally derived from the Greek Καθαρὸς, "pure," but all the earliest writers call her, not *Katherina*, but Αἰχατερίνη or Αἰχατερίνα, or Æcaterina. This is still the name of the saint in the Greek Church, and towns are called after her, as Ekaterinoslav, Ekaterinograd.   If Katherina or Katharina be the original spelling, the prefix Αἰ or Æ is unaccounted for.   In 1755 Falconius, Archbishop of San Severino, throws overboard the whole legend of the Alexandrian martyr, and suggests that she and her name are variants of Ἡχαριτίνα, or Ἡχαρτερία, or of Saint Barbara.*

There is no known mention of Saint Katherine in writing before the ninth century. Catholic martyrologists can only suggest that she is the unnamed Christian lady spoken of by Eusebius.† Rufinus, the translator of Eusebius, says that this lady was Dorothea, and avers that she was not slain, but exiled under the Emperor Maximin. At the end

* *The Life and Martyrdom of Saint Katherine of Alexandria.* See Mr. Henry Hucks Gibb's preface to the edition of the Roxburghe Club, 1884.

† Hist. Eccl., lib. viii. 14.

of the fourth century, in which Katherine is said to have lived, Heraclides wrote his *Paradisus* to commemorate saintly women of Egypt; but about Katherine he has nothing to say. In 1680 the Archbishop of Paris, revising the Paris breviary, removed Saint Katherine from the calendar. It is difficult to believe that her legend sprang from nothing at all but the remark of Eusebius, "a certain Christian lady was banished by Maximin for her obstinate virtue." When we next meet with the tale of Saint Katherine, it is five hundred years later, in the *Menologium Basilianum* of the ninth century. The author says that Æcaterina, daughter of a prince in

24

Alexandria, rebuked the Emperor Maximin for idolatry; that he sent for fifty sophists to reason with her; that she converted them; that they were burned, and that she was beheaded. In the following century, the tenth, the legend has grown in the hands of Symeon Metaphrastes; and finally we learn that Katherine was condemned to death on a spiked wheel (her emblem in art); that the wheel, split by an angel, slew four thousand pagans; that Katherine was beheaded, and that angels carried her body to Mount Sinai, where some of her relics yet remain. Still later appears the story of Saint Katherine's wedlock with our Lord, though, if we know anything at all about paradise, it is that *there* is no marrying or giving in marriage. Saint Katherine is commemorated on November 25th; she wears the red crown of martyrdom, the blue crown of preachers, and the white crown of virgins.

That she beheld the saint crowned, Jeanne d'Arc attested, but absolutely refused to give any other details as to her costume and appearance. In the old English life of Saint Katherine—the extant manuscript was written about 1430—we are told that when the saint was imprisoned by the pagan emperor "the Archangel Mychael came to counfort her" . . . and that "the place where she was kept closed shone wyth a merueylous lyght." In the very year when the scribe wrote these words, the English thrust into a dungeon that new saint and martyr, La Pucelle, whom Saint Michael comforted as he did Saint Katherine. To Jeanne, as to her real or fabled Alexandrian patroness and prototype, Saint Michael said, in the words of the old English author, " Drede not, thou mayden acceptable to God, bot worke sadly and myghtyly, for our Lord ys wyth thee for whos worschep thou hast entered into this batayle: he schal give into thy mouth the stronge flood of hys plenteous word to the whyche thyn aduersaries schal not wythstonde, ... and thou wythynne short whyle after schalt ende thy batayle wyth glorious deeth, and be so receyved amonge the worthy company of virgyns." The angel thus spoke on the eve of Saint Katherine's encounter in argument with the fifty sophists of the pagan emperor. The struggle of Jeanne d'Arc with the crowd of ecclesiastical sophists who were bent on her destruction offers a singular parallel to the trial of Saint Katherine.

And to Jeanne also in prison in 1430–31, as to Saint Katherine in the old English life then a-writing, came the angel and the voice, the promise of help to withstand her judges, the promise of release from martyrdom and of entrance into paradise. It may well be that the Maid had heard this incident in the legend of Saint Katherine narrated; and even if the old legend be mythical, its echo in the heart of Jeanne rendered her strong to endure, to believe, and to "end her battle by glorious death." Before Saint Katherine's own death, as recounted in our old English legend, a voice from heaven bade her be comforted: "And to them that in perels and nedes calle unto the I behote from heuene. hasty and desyred help." As for the bringing of her relics into France, the English legend assigns it to "a Monke of the Cyte of Roue that ys in Normandye"—that is,

Rouen, where the servant of Saint Katherine was burned in 1431. The relics were really carried from Sinai to Richard II of Normandy by one Simon, a monk; but Richard was dead before they arrived.

Of Fierbois, the shrine there, and the then recent miracles recorded in the chapel register, the old English Life says nothing. Perhaps the author, using a Latin original, knew not of them; perhaps he had no pleasure in miracles wrought for a hostile race. Yet Philip the Good,— so-called,— of Burgundy, who gave up Jeanne d'Arc to the death of fire, was himself a devotee of Saint Katherine, and commanded his secretary, Jean Mielot, to write her life. As if the saint were to be a reconciler of political and religious animosities, Dr. Eugen Einenkel has guessed that her legend is founded on no Christian martyrdom, but on the life and death of the beautiful and learned Hypatia, a theory in which he unconsciously followed Mrs. Jamieson. Hypatia and Saint Katherine, to be sure, were both of them maidens of Alexandria; both were noble, erudite, and holy of life; both died for their irreconcilable creeds; and both, as maidens and martyrs, were fit examples to Jeanne d'Arc. But the piety of the middle ages would have hotly resented the hypothesis that churches were dedicated to and miracles were wrought by Hypatia, an incorrigible woman of heathendom.

Saint Katherine of Alexandria, the patroness of Fierbois, is, then, a shadowy historical figure. The known evidence is certainly not sufficient to prove that she ever existed at all, and her legend swells into marvelous and romantic dimensions before our eyes. Between the ninth century *Menologium*, our earliest document, and a Latin text of the legend, written in the eleventh century, there is an extraordinary growth of the miraculous. Whether the tale of the fifty converted sophists, of the cruel wheel, of the decapitation, of the angelic translation of the saint's body from Alexandria to Sinai, was developed between the ninth and eleventh centuries, or was only borrowed in the latter age, from Sinaitic tradition, we need not pause to inquire. It is enough that we have no sound or documentary evidence about the real history, or even about the existence, of Saint Katherine.

The obvious and natural inference is that the devout, in the middle ages, prayed to, attributed miracles to, and—in the case of Jeanne d'Arc—actually saw and spoke with a dead woman who probably never was a living woman. At that point the rough and ready methods of scepticism are likely to leave the inquiry, probably not without a parting jeer. Our ancestors were a

set of darkened bigots, taking imag-
inations for actualities, and living in
fantasy. An age of scientific en-
lightenment has only to thank
"whatever gods there be" that it is
not as other ages were, nor even as
these ancestors of ours.

This is the view of popular science,
whose professors and lecturers may
deign to throw in (as parallels to the
Maid) a few stock examples of hal-
lucinated patients, such as the un-
ceasing Nicolaï and "Mrs. A." But,
if we are to be really scientific, if we
are really to exercise a judicious curi-
osity about human nature and human
faculty, in the past and present, we
cannot so lightly dismiss even these
miracles of Madame Saint Katherine

of Fierbois. By listening to and obeying the voice of Saint Katherine a peasant girl changed the face of Europe and the fates of kingdoms. An influence which was thus obeyed is not a thing to be superciliously neglected. Again, the facts of human nature are matters worthy of observation, and among these facts the persistent repetition of thanks for miraculous deliverances claim our attention.

How is the fact that the stories in the following collection were told, to be explained? That they are mere forgeries of priests, for the purpose of drawing pilgrims and gifts to Fierbois, is a theory which satisfied the scepticism of the eighteenth century. To refute it is not possible, for lack of documents, but perhaps the majority of readers find it no longer credible. Persons often of noted eminence and others of honorable position would scarcely have allowed this shameless use to be made of their names. The cynicism of the whole proceeding is too audacious. Nor can we suppose that all the witnesses made journeys, often long, perilous, and costly, merely to tell lies. In a number of cases the pilgrims probably believed in their own stories; indeed, several of these stories are even now credible, containing no element of the marvelous. A captive, after prayer to Saint Katherine, picks up courage enough to knock down his captor at a dangerous point of a hill pass; or he conceives a stratagem which had not occurred to him before; or he finds a knife or a file, and does not know how to account for their presence, except by the grace of Madame Saint Katherine. Here there is no touch of the marvelous, the introduction of the word "miracle" is due to the gratitude and the devout imagination of the delivered prisoner. Again, where the rope fails to hang a man, as in two or three stories, we may conceive that the amateur hangsman was not an expert. If the patient feels himself lifted up and supported, while hanging, by invisible hands, *that* may be a mere subjective sensation, though certainly not experienced by modern culprits who have been half hanged. As to miracles of healing, these (it is now generally acknowledged) may be wrought to an undefined extent by what we call " imagination," or " suggestion," which our ignorant fathers called *Faith*.

But other reported events, more startling than these, occur frequently. Doors open of their own accord. The irons fall from the limbs of the devout. Men are bodily "levitated," they know not how; and one, falling asleep in prison, awakes to find himself still in irons, in the hall of his own house! Another is "supernaturally" raised up to the level of a window set high in the wall, and for him the locks and bars of his *huche*, or cage, had already undone themselves, he knew not how.

We may, as before, assert that these witnesses, at least, were lying and knew it. Perhaps they were. We do not gain much by observing, what is perfectly true, that the undoing of bonds and opening of doors is a feature of miracle common to the Bible and to savage necromancy as well as to modern conjuring. In the life of Thomas Atkinson, a priest, hanged at York in 1616, we read of "that extraordinary event, the irons falling off his legs when he was employed in prayer, a thing well known and attested by many."* In brief, all the miracles of the Fierbois register have their parallels, not only in the religious records of the world, but in the feats attributed to D. D. Home, to Highland second-sighted men, Hebrew prophets, and Australian *biraarks*. The evidence is of every degree of excellence or badness, from the signed testimony of Fellows of the Royal Society, and Continental savants, to the gossip of Celtic gillies; the value of the evidence varies, but not the nature of the alleged facts. And while the alleged facts remain identical, or analogous, the supposed causes of

* See Chaloner's *British Martyrology*, ii. 55.

the facts vary with the belief of the narrator. Hartmann and Aksakoff make their guesses; spiritualists and savages hold by "spirits"; a little exact observation detects common sleight-of-hand in the childish tricks of modern paid impostors; the Catholic narrators allege in the Fierbois cases "the grace of God, granted at the prayer of Madame Saint Katherine."

Here we may leave the puzzle *why these narratives concerning miracles were told.* That the abnormal facts reported really occurred, we are not maintaining; still less do we maintain that Saint Katherine of Alexandria had a hand in them. We only observe that to tell such tales, often apparently in good faith, is a persistent factor in human character. A Catholic age gave them a Catholic coloring, that is all.

If human nature, in different ages, varies little as regards the startling stories which it delights to tell, there occur great changes in superficial matters. War is war and a curse, everywhere, but our present records add fresh proof of the barbarity with which war was waged in the ages of Monstrelet and Froissart. The English in France, the Burgundians, the Scots, the companies of ill-paid mercenaries lived by plunder, and by extorting ransoms from prisoners taken in battle, or seized among the fields, or in front of their own mills,

like one devotee of Saint Katherine.
If no ransom, or no adequate ransom,
was promised, the head of the prisoner was cut off, or he was hanged.
Probably the indignation caused by
Jeanne d'Arc, when she allowed a
robber knight, Franquet d'Arras, to
be tried and executed at Lagny, was
aroused because Franquet was ready
and willing to pay ransom. Certainly captive men at arms, and even
knights, were often slain out of hand,
in the takings of castles, as our
records prove. These men may
have been unable or unwilling to
ransom themselves.

Captives were cruelly treated;
we hear of one obliged to run beside
his captor's horse till he asked to be

slain. Others are thrown ironed into damp ditches and cellars, or have chains placed on their arms while their legs are fixed in heavy *seps*, a kind of iron stocks. Hunger, disease, and suffering prey upon victims thus burdened, or inclosed (as Jeanne d'Arc was on her way to Rouen) in cages (*huches*).* This extreme form of savagery was nothing strange or rare: we read about it frequently in the Fierbois register. That a woman might be treated with this rigor, even when no charge of sorcery or of ordinary crime was brought against her, we gather from the case (here recorded) of Margarite de Monnay

* There is a wooden cage, or *huche*, for securing a prisoner at Canterbury.

(1437). She was kept for five years by the English, and though imprisoned merely as a pledge for her husband's ransom, she was held in iron bonds, and, at night, was in the *sep*, while no woman was in attendance on her. Thus the treatment of Jeanne d'Arc at Rouen, incredibly base and cruel as it seems to us, was not unfamiliar to the manners of the English, at least, in that so-called age of chivalry. To extort money from prisoners by brutal usage was the aim and end of giving quarter. War was organized brigandage.

As an example of the system of ransom, we may take the case of Jehan du Chastel, who, on June 6, 1428, before the siege of Orléans

began, made his pilgrimage to Fierbois.   Jehan had sallied from Ven-
dôme, with Regnault Guillaume, brother of the celebrated La Hire, and
other men-at-arms. Seeing La Hire's
brother in peril, Jehan rode to his
rescue, but was seized by an Englishman, "John the Painter." "*Rends
toy !* " said the Englishman, and Jehan said "*je me rends,*" but did not
add, " on my faith," or " rescue or
no rescue."   Rescued he was and
rode away, but the Englishman later
summoned him to give himself up,
and, on his refusal, challenged him
to single combat.   They fought in
the lists, the Frenchman (who had
made his vow to Saint Katherine)
was the victor, and he appeared at

Fierbois to thank the Saint, arrayed in the armor of his enemy. To the truth of his tale, destitute as it is of marvel, witness was borne by Monseigneur the Bastard of Orléans, by the famed La Hire, and several others.

Perhaps the quaintest of all the stories is that which Michael Hamilton told on May 4, 1429. If he was able to march (which seems doubtful) he ought not to have been at Fierbois on that day, but fighting at Orléans under Ogilvie, Chambers, or Kennedy, the Scottish comrades of La Pucelle, for the love of the Maid and of chivalry. This Michael, whose evidence was so sensational that hundreds of people came to hear it, was born in a Scottish parish dedicated to Saint Katherine. About such parishes Mr. Hay Fleming writes to me :

" There was a chapel of St. Catherine in the burying-ground of Kilbarchan (seven or eight miles almost due south of Dumbarton). It is mentioned in the Acts of Parliament, x. 97b. But the name of the parish, as Cosmo Innes says, implies that it was dedicated to Saint Barchan. In one of its villages there is also a chapel to Saint Bride (*Origines Parochiales*, Ban. Club, i. 84), so I fear that parish will hardly do.

" In the parish of Bothwell there was also a chapel dedicated to Saint Katherine ; and it seems that it was

Miracles of Saint Katherine

the part of the parish containing this chapel which was soon after the Reformation erected into a separate parish under the name of Shotts, Bartram Shotts, or Bothwell Minor, the chapel being then used as the parish church. See Scott's *Fasti*, ii. 297 ; Hamilton's *Lanark and Renfrew*, Mait. Club, p. 38 ; *Origines Parochiales*, i. 53, 54. Shotts should surely do ! "

Let us make it Shotts then, and congratulate Lanarkshire on having produced a narrator whose vigor of style and obvious delight in his tale distinguish him among his French allies. Another Scottish devotee, John Fary, held the pleasing post of King's minstrel, and is one of the

7 49

few whose votive offering is mentioned. His was a human head fashioned in wax, with the very arrow sticking in it which had wounded himself.

Among celebrated persons mentioned in the register are not only La Hire and Dunois, but de Gaucourt, who opposed Jeanne d'Arc when she wished to sally forth and attack the English at Les Tourelles, on May 7, 1429. He was also with her when she was wounded in her assault on Paris, in the same year. Gaucourt only appears incidentally, as captain of a company of whom one lost six silver cups at an inn, cups miraculously recovered. The Scottish practice of Jeddart justice is illustrated in 1423, when some Scots who had been robbed in a certain district hanged Jehan de Pons and other sportsmen before going through the formality of trying them. The adventure of Jehan Moreau (1437) illustrates the respect entertained for sanctuaries, though it was not strong enough to protect a certain unlucky Breton.

Such are the traits of life and manners which the Fierbois register yields, grains of historical gold in the confused strata of not very plausible reports. A French priest has suggested that Fierbois might renew its fame and become the rival of Lourdes. If Saint Katherine deigned to appear at Fierbois this result would probably follow, but modern pilgrims are led thither chiefly by devotion to a saint more authentic and more recent than the learned lady of Alexandria,— by love of La Pucelle.*

* The register contains some thirty miracles more recent than those included in the Abbé Bourassé's collection, but in no case are the devotees Scottish.

THE MIRACLES

I

THE YEAR 1375

HE year one thousand three hundred sixty and fifteen, it befell that when as Hylaire Habert, of the parish of Saint Espain, was building the chapel of Madame Saint Katherine of Fierboys, the thing that he did sorely displeased his wife. And she was even too much cumbered for that he would build the said chapel, and left his business to do the same.

Therefore prayed his wife to God that he might never return nor come again to his own house. And it so befell her that she dropped down as one dead, her eyes and mouth shut, *sans* speech or movement, being as stiff as a stick, nor ever returned to herself, till her lord came from the said chapel. And at this point he found her, who thereon took a vow for her to Madame Saint Katherine, and promised to bring his wife to that saint, if Madame would restore her, whole and well. So soon as he had done his prayer, she opened her eyes and began to speak, and was as well as ever she had been. And straightway he led her to the said chapel, and there made she her oblation, and so departed, whole and well.

II

THE YEAR 1380

ATURDAY, vigil of Pentecost, **one thousand three hundred and eighty, Perrot Chapon,** of the Parish of Saint Salvator near Luzarche, came to the chapel to submit himself thankfully to Madame Saint Katherine, acknowledging the grace that she won from him of Our Lord; namely, the delivery of his body that was held of the English in chains; and there was he for a whole month in irons, nor no deliverance could he find for himself.

8   57

So made he his vow to Madame Saint Katherine, that if he might escape without paying ransom, verily he would go on pilgrimage to her · chapel. And no sooner was his vow made in prison — his wife also making her vow about that same hour,— than he fell asleep, and on his waking, lo, he was in the hall of his own house, all in chains of iron as he was. And so hath he come to the chapel, to give thanks to Our Lord, and to the Virgin, and hath sworn that this is true.

III

THE YEAR 1383

HE year of grace one thousand three hundred eighty and three, the Tuesday after Easter, came into the chapel here Clement de la Biere, of the diocese of Xaintes, near la Rochelle, and of the parish of Estre, who since Christmas was taken prisoner of the English in Chaluceau, he and divers others.

And when they were taken, the same Clement was right strongly bound with his arms behind his back, and his feet made fast beneath the belly of a horse he had. And when Clement found himself hard by the keep of the English, then called he on Madame Saint Katherine, and made his vow to go on pilgrimage to her chapel here, before Pentecost, if but she would deliver him from bonds. And so soon as his vows were made the cords wherewith he was bound fell to earth, and he rode off with his horse safe and sound, though verily he who should have warded him told the English that this prisoner was escaping. And to this he maketh oath.

Present, Guillaume Le Fournier of the said parish, Guillaume Tricot, and others.

IV

THE YEAR 1383

HE year of grace one thousand three hundred eighty and three, the Saturday after Easter, came into the chapel here Guillaume Oade, a Welshman, declaring and affirming by his faith and oath, that, in the foregoing year, between All Saints and Christmas, three days before the battle which our lord the King fought in Flanders, whereof he had the victory over the Flemings and folk rebellious, he, Guillaume Oade, was lodged at Poperigue in Flanders,

two leagues and a half from Ipre,
with great company of men-at-arms.
They, on a Saturday about midnight,
went forth of their lodgings and out
of Poperigue, after setting fire to the
town in all quarters. Now in that
hour the said Guillaume and his varlet
were sleeping in the house whereas
they lodged. And when the men-
at-arms had departed, thither came
great company of Flemings and of
men-at-arms of their party, so that
the whole town was full of them.
Whereon the said Guillaume and his
varlet, hearing the uproar of them,
went forth from the house, thinking
to flee, and they called on Madame
Saint Katherine of Fierboys, to whom
Guillaume made his vow.

Then folk ran in on them from every quarter, but the varlet fled and escaped by his speed, and by grace of God and Madame Saint Katherine.

And the said Guillaume, who saw that he might neither fight nor flee, ran into a thatched house, and these Flemings knew not what had become of him. And he clomb into the roof of that house, and was there till morning. And when the fire had burned all the houses thereabout, the said Guillaume, seeing all the houses fall flaming against his, and the fire entering at front and rear, made his vow yet again to Madame Saint Katherine of Fierboys.

Then sallied he forth thereof, and
thought to get him gone. So met he
Flemings who ran in on him from
all sides, so that the said Guillaume
might not avail to flee further. So
he leaped into a great river and deep,
if at all he might escape death, and
sank to the bottom. And when he
arose again, he betook himself to
swimming, and so passed to the
other side of that river. But he was
scarce come forth of the water, when
he was taken of Flemings, that cut
and seized his purse and his money,
which hung from his neck. And
seeing that they thought to smite
and slay him with axes and pikes,
he prayed yet again to Madame
Saint Katherine, and so escaped

forth from among them. And so abode three days, till he could find them of his own party, during which three days he met Flemings in other places, who did him no manner of mischief.

SINE ANNO

HE Tuesday before the Translation of Saint Martin, there were in the chapel here four men of a village near the parish of La Souterraine, where they were taken by English men-at-arms of a garrison lodged within six leagues of La Souterraine; and the said four men were carried by the English within their said hold. There the English bound them as straitly, as they might, and beat them sorely, and so went to dinner. Then the prisoners with one

voice vowed themselves to Madame Saint Katherine, namely that, if it pleased her they should escape unharmed and without ransom from the said prison, they would visit her in her chapel of Fierboys and there make oblations. Then straightway the bonds wherewith they were bound fell from their hands and feet, and they came forth of that hold, into the court, and issued out by the gate, which they found open, neither the porter nor any of those within saying them nay. And they met the men-at-arms who had been at their taking, who knew them not and said no word to them, nor wrought them any harm, but went into their own lodgings. And to accomplish their vows to Madame Saint Katherine, they came hither together, the Saturday after the Octave of the Translation of Saint Martin, they, their wives, and children, and swore and affirmed that the said tale is true, making oath in the presence of several notable persons come on pilgrimage from Vendome to the chapel.

VI

THE YEAR 1410

HE Friday before the Magdalene, in the year one thousand four hundred and ten, came on pilgrimage to the chapel here a man named Thomas du Mont, for whom, and for another named Perrinet l'Auvergnat, God wrought, at the prayer of Our Lady and of Madame Saint Katherine, a right noble and evident miracle.

These two men were taken between Paris and Montleheri, by Burgundians from Rousselet and Ferreboue. Thence were they taken to

Corbail, and there cast with three others into a fosse, narrow and as deep as a lance's length, and above them was laid a right great rock, that they might not avail to win forth.

There were they kept straitly, and so lay for full fourteen months and three days, being put at so great ransom that all their friends would have been over hard-set to pay it. And because they would not pay, they were kept on bread and water right straitly during the said time of fourteen months and three days, so hardly, and in such sort that their three fellows died in the fosse, and now it was full eight days since the last of them died, whereby the said

Thomas and Perrinet suffered sore from the filth and the stench.

Right so prayed they devoutly to the Virgin Mary and Madame Saint Katherine of Fierboys, that it would please God to free them from forth of that filth, wherein they lay. So set they them on their knees, with their faces turned as straight as they might towards the chapel of Madame Saint Katherine of Fierboys, and thither they vowed that they would make pilgrimage so soon as they might, after they were escaped.

Now straightway, their vow being paid, they fell on sleep, and when they woke they found themselves above the fosse, and the rock rolled away as it were two turns, the said rock being so heavy that it needed two men to turn it over. And the said fosse was in the tower of Corbail, where Seine water forks. So found they a boat and crossed the water safe and sound. Thence went they to Montleheri, and there died Perrinet l'Auvergnat, of the pestilence they had taken in prison, he being yet minded to achieve his pilgrimage. But the said Thomas lay long sick ere he could achieve his pilgrimage. And he hath said and borne witness by the faith of his body that the thing is true, in the presence of Jehan Chermeteau, warden of the said chapel, and of many other persons.

VII

THE YEAR 1414

HE year one thousand and four hundred and fourteen, the Thursday after the Purification of Our Lady, there passed by the Pont de Ruen the Sieur de Gaucourt and Remouet de la Guerce, having with them a great company of men-at-arms. And a man-at-arms left in the house of Jehan de Balan and Loyse his wife a casket which he forgot at the said house, wherein were six cups of silver. Now these cups had certain folk taken and carried

away thefteously, Balan and his wife knowing nothing thereof. Right so came the said man-at-arms, after that day, to the house, demanding his gear from Jehan de Balan and his wife. Then were they right dolorous and cumbered, for the man-at-arms was for laying them under sore duresse to render up his goods. True it is that when the woman saw that perforce she must render back the casket, or that she and her husband should suffer heavy loss, she knew not what to do, nor might find any remede. Save only that she commended herself to God, to Our Lady, and to Madame Saint Katherine of Fierboys, promising and vowing that if Madame would be pleased to pray God for her, and if by her intercession the cups were found, she would travel barefoot to the chapel in this place. So came she, as she had vowed, to this chapel, and let sing a Mass. Right so, the Mass being ended, news came to her in the said chapel, that the casket and cups were found. And true it is that in the night on which she set forth, in the evening, the cups were brought into the church of Pont de Ruen, and were found there in the morning, and the thing was approven by several witnesses.

VIII

THE YEAR 1418

HE year one thousand four hundred and eighteen, a gentleman following the wars, named Casin du Boys, was in garrison in the castle of Beaumont on Oyse, which castle the Duke of Burgundy assaulted, and the assault endured three days and three nights, and the castle was taken by force, whereon they cut off the heads of twenty gentlemen who were within that castle. And therein were Casin and divers others.

Now this Casin was taken and

carried to a village some two leagues from Beaumont, and there was shut up in a case locked with a key, bound moreover was the said cage with a right strong rope all about it, and he who took Casin was minded to cut off his head, so he heard. And a man was bidden to lie above the cage, that Casin might find no manner of means to issue forth and escape.

So befell it that Casin, being inclosed in that cage, and knowing himself in peril of death, bethought him of the great and virtuous miracles which God wrought at the prayer of the glorious virgin, Madame Saint Katherine of Fierboys, and of the noble pilgrimage to her chapel. Therefore he made his vows to Madame Saint Katherine, imploring her to be pleased to aid him with God, in such sort that he might escape, whereon he would straightway betake himself in pilgrimage to the chapel of Fierboys.

Right so, his vow being made, and his prayer, the said cage flew open of its own accord, and forth went Casin, he that lay above the cage perceiving naught. Now he that had taken Casin slept in the same chamber, with his *chamberière*, neither heard they anything.

And when Casin was forth of the cage, no manner could he find whereby he might issue from the house. Then looked he up at a window that was set the height of two men from the ground, or thereby, so high that he might not reach it, nor found no means to climb to it. So prayed he again to Madame Saint Katherine that as by virtue of her prayer he was issued forth from the cage, so also it would please her to set him forth of the house. Right so, his prayer being ended, he found his breast on a level with the window, and him seemed that he was hoven under the armpits. Then went he forth of the house, and so to Creil, and passed many stations of Burgundian men-at-arms, and drank and ate with them, and they never misdoubted him. And to the truth of this he has sworn, by the faith and oath of his body.

IX

THE YEAR 1421

HE Friday after Michaelmas, one thousand four hundred and twenty-one, Guillaume Guy, a squire, native of Piregort, was taken by the English at Rogemont in the Beauce, between Acheres and Blevies, who carried him into the Fauxbourgs of Pontoyse, and held him to ransom at fifty crowns of gold, which ransom they bade him pay or release two English prisoners. Then put they him endlong in a barrel, and shut him up therein, and above laid

two great tables, and an Englishman lay on the tables.

In the night the squire vowed him to Madame Saint Katherine, praying her to pray God to deliver him. And about midnight he found the tables scattered apart, one above, one below, and the Englishman sleeping on the ground. Then came he forth of the barrel, and escaped safe and sound, by grace of God and of Madame Saint Katherine; as also report Thomas Rouvallet, squire, Jehan Fardeau, and Clement l'Evesque, all of the fellowship of Alain Giron, who have said and sworn on oath that these things are true.

X

THE YEAR 1423

HE twenty-fourth of the month of April, in the year one thousand four hundred and twenty-three, there came into the chapel here one named Perrin Gougeaut, of the parish of Saint Germain de Relez, who had been taken by Burgundians the Sunday before, in the evening about sunset. There were seven Burgundians at his taking, who took along with him another man called Noriceté Girart, and bound them and coupled them together, and espe-

cially the said Perrin was bound with four ropes right straitly. Then made they their vows to Madame Saint Katherine of Fierboys. And instantly their vows being made, they found themselves all unbound before the very eyes of the Burgundians, who wrought them no harm nor annoy.

Then went they and laid them down in a wood, and there slept, and so escaped.

That this is true the said Perrin has sworn by the faith of his body, with these present, Guillaume Tallebot, Perrin Briant, Brother Gilles Lecourt, and many others.

XI

THE YEAR 1423

HE sixth day of the month of May of the year one thousand four hundred and twenty-three, Guillaume Bressin, native of Saint-Brieuc in Bretagne, came into the chapel here, who about Michaelmas last had been taken by the English. And he was carried to Rouen and put in the fosse in irons, he and another with him. And the other went free and the said Bressin remained as a hostage for both. Now the other was

84

to return and bring back a ransom for both of them. But he returned not, nor came nor sent. Therefore the said Bressin lay in prison for the space of seventeen weeks. Then he, being in great heaviness, remembered him of the Virgin Mary, and of Madame Saint Katherine of Fierboys, to whom he made his vow. And his vow being done and his orison, straightway the English struck off his irons, and set him free out of the ditch. Thereon he departed from them and escaped out of their hands, and went away without ransom, no man harming him.

And the said Bressin firmly believes that he would never have escaped, save for the intercession of the Virgin Mary and Madame Saint Katherine.

And that this is true he has sworn by the faith of his body, in the presence of Messire Kyrthrizien, warden of the said chapel, of Messire Jehan Bredar, and several other persons.

XII

THE YEAR 1423

HE eleventh day of June, in the year one thousand four hundred and twenty-three, Jehan de Pons, of the parish of Masuet in Berry, came into the chapel here to accomplish his vow. He had been taken on the sixth day of the said month, by Scots, in the country of Berry, as he was hunting partridges on the said sixth day of June, in a field of wheat, and had with him seven laborers, and all seven were taken with him by the said Scots, who had been

robbed in that country by brigands. Then the Scots led all eight of them to an oak tree and there hanged the seven to the said oak tree, that they died.

Then remained the said Jehan the last to be hanged, because he had prayed for this grace in God's name to him that took him, to this end, that he might have time and space to pray God's mercy and pardon.

There saw he all these seven hanged and strangled before his eyes.

Therefore made he his vow devoutly to Madame Saint Katherine of Fierboys that it would please her to implore the grace of our Creator towards him.

Then was he hanged the last, right high on the said oak tree, by a halter that was almost new. And when he that hanged <u>him</u> was mounted and riding after the others, being now about a bow-shot from the said oak, the halter wherewith Jehan was hanged broke asunder, and he fell on a heap of sharp stones, harming himself no more than if it had been on a pillow, and he felt no pain when he was hanged up, for it seemed that one hove him up under the feet. So came he to accomplish his vow in the year and date above written, and to thank Madame Saint Katherine in her chapel of Fierboys, bringing with him the broken halter. Moreover he swore by the faith of his body that this had befallen him in the form and manner before said in the presence of Brother Jehan Chermeteau, as then warden of the said chapel, Monsieur Nicolas Raou, Brother Gilles Lecourt, Monsieur Pierre Trincart, and several others.

XIII

THE YEAR 1425

HE thirteenth day of January, the year one thousand four hundred and twenty-five, came on pilgrimage to-day to the chapel of Madame Saint Katherine of Fierboys Jehan Ducoudray, a native of Saumur, and Jehan Courtin of the parish of Argentre near Laval Guion, who related and revealed the miracles which follow.

It is to be known that on Christmas eve last they escaped from the prison of the English wherein they lay within the castle of Belesme.

There had they lain, Ducoudray
for three years and a half, and Courtin since the day of Verneuil fight,
and were in company of several
others in strong prison, some ironed,
some bound. And they had more
times than once essayed to escape,
but could find no remede by no manner or means. So they all made their
vows to Madame Saint Katherine on
that Christmas eve, and especially
the said Jehan Ducoudray and Jehan Courtin promised to come on
pilgrimage to her chapel, so soon as
they might, after escaping from prison. And on Christmas eve, their
prayer being made to Madame Saint
Katherine, they broke hold, and
came before the gaoler, who cried

out so loud that all the town was astir. Then clomb Jehan Ducoudray first on to the wall of the town, and met the sentinel, who seized him. Then Jehan threw the sentinel over the wall, and bade his own fellows be no whit dismayed, but put their trust in Madame Saint Katherine, that she would be their succour. So let they themselves slip from the wall into the ditch, and escaped by grace of God and of Madame Saint Katherine, and that wall was about the height of two lances.

This they have sworn to be true by the faith of their bodies, in presence of Messire Richard Kyrthrizian, warden of the said chapel, of Robert Cornabel, and several others.

XIV

THE YEAR 1425

N the aforesaid year and day (January the thirteenth, one thousand four hundred and twenty-five) came on pilgrimage to the chapel a gentleman named Jehan Godelin, of the parish of Besse in Braie, who was taken by the English on mid-August day, in the year passed. And next day was he led to the gibbet, with six of his fellows, all six being hanged before his eyes on the said gibbet.

Now even when he saw the first

of the six hanged, he made his vow
to Madame Saint Katherine, praying
her that she would be pleased to rescue him from such shameful death.
So abode he, and was led away, none
harming him, and was held to ransom. And hath sworn the faith of his
body that this is true. Present, the
aforesaid Messire Richard, and Cornabel, and divers other persons.

XV

THE YEAR 1425

HE fifth day of February, in the year one thousand four hundred and twenty-five, came Jehan Hurpois of La Chartre sur Lair, on pilgrimage to the chapel of Madame Saint Katherine of Fierboys. He had been made prisoner by the English, at La Chartre, when they took the town, and he made his vow to Madame Saint Katherine when he saw the English in that place. So took they the city, and slew many, but him they harmed not, save that they put

him in cages, in irons, and in strong
prison. Thereafter, when they led
him to Alençon, they made him
run beside their horses all the way.
Thereby was he so wearied, that in
no manner might he go further, and
so desired death rather than life, and
said to his master who led him :

" My master, I pray and beseech
you, since other grace you will not
do me, that you will be pleased to
send me out of this world and this
life."

Then said the Englishman to him,"
"since you are fain to die, I will slay
you shortly."

So haled he the man behind a
bush, and drew his naked sword.
Then Jehan kneeled down, and de-

voutly prayed Madame Saint Katherine that of her grace she would be his comfort. And anon the Englishman struck him thrice as hard as strike he could, on his naked neck, yet cut him not, nor wounded him, nor did him no manner of harm. And when the Englishman perceived that he had wounded him not at all, he left him, and called another Englishman who had a led horse, and mounted Jehan thereon.

The said Jehan saith that afterwards he heard the Englishman say that when he had struck the three strokes, and saw that there was no wound, he remembered him of Madame Saint Katherine, and well deemed that Jehan had recommended himself to her, and so he had pity on Jehan.

So was he led to Alençon. And when Le Mans was taken, he was led thither, and escaped without ransom, by prayer and power of the glorious Virgin, Madame Saint Katherine. And by the faith of his body hath Jehan sworn that all this is true, in presence of Messire Richard Kyrthrizian, Brother Gilles Lacour, warders of this chapel, and several others.

XVIII

THE YEAR 1429

HE fourth day of May, in the year one thousand four hundred and twenty-nine, did Michael Hamilton, a Scot, esquire of the company of John Stewart, captain, present himself in the chapel of Madame Saint Katherine of Fierboys. Who swore on his oath that the miracle following is true. It is to be known that right willingly with all his power and strength he has ever served, with all his heart and devotion, the glorious Virgin Mary and

Madame Saint Katherine. And even says that the parish wherein he was born was founded in the honor of Madame Saint Katherine, wherefore, for honor and remembrance of her, since he has come into France, with true heart and devout he has made pilgrimage to seek her in her chapel of Fierboys.

He says that last Holy Week he and several foot-soldiers at arms were lodged in Brittany, in a village called Calletz, near Clisson. And he saith that on a certain day the Bretons were of force in the fields, and wished to rob the said Scots, wherefore they sent a certain spy to search out their lodgings. This spy the Scots took and questioned him, and learned from him that the Bretons were minded to seize them. And after they had learned what they could from the said spy they hanged him. Then such of the Scots as could flee departed. But the Bretons came up and took and slew those whom they found, and among others they took the said Hamilton, who could not flee for the weight of his armor, and led him to Clisson. Thereon the son of the spy who had been hanged seized Michael, and vowed that he would hang him for the love of his father. And in truth before the eyes of the other Bretons and with their good-will, he bound Michael's hands behind his back, and hanged him from the gibbet of Clisson in his shirt, hose, and shoon. There was he hanged on Munday Thursday, two hours after noon. This being done, they departed.

Nevertheless the said Hamilton so soon as he was taken did nothing but think devoutly of Madame Saint Katherine, and prayed that she would be pleased to guard him from death, whereon he would come humbly to thank her in her chapel of Fierboys. So prayed he more than once or twice.

So chanced it that, when he had been hanged, there came a voice to the curé of the town bidding him go speedily and cut down Hamilton. Of this voice the curé took no keep, and forgot it until the morrow, which was Good Friday. And when the said curé had done all his service it was near noon. Then he bethought him of the said voice, and bade one of his parish go to the gibbet and see if Hamilton were dead or not, and bring him back the truth thereof. Wherefore the man went on that errand. And when he got thither he turned and spun the Scotsman about, and knew not whether he was dead or alive.

Nevertheless, to know the very truth, he took the hose from the right foot and slit the little toe with a knife, so that therein was a great wound and much blood. And when the said Hamilton felt it, he swears by his oath that as long as he was hanging he felt no harm, no more than if he had been hanged by a rope under his arms. For when he was hanged he kept praying Madame Saint Katherine to be his aid, without other thought. And it seems him that he was hoven up under his feet. Nevertheless, when he felt the wound in his said toe, he drew up his leg and stirred. Thereon sore fear and terror fell on the messenger of the curé, as Hamilton hath since heard him say. Wherefore he ran hastily to the curé, declaring that Hamilton was still alive and he had seen him move. Then the said curé considering his voice in the night, and considering that Hamilton had been hanged from Maundy

Thursday to Good Friday afternoon, deemed that it was evident miracle, and proclaimed all these things to the people present. Whereafter he and the other people of holy church put on their vestments and with a great company they went to the gibbet, and cut down the said Hamilton. And when he was let down, all they that stood by saw that it was a miracle of God, and whileas they looked at him, he moved. Now he that had hanged him was present, who, in wrath that he was not dead, struck him over the ear with a sword, and gave him a great wound, for which he was blamed. Nevertheless the said Hamilton was set on a horse, and taken into a house to be nursed and cared for. But a noble lady, the Abbess of La Regrepiere, heard of the miracle and sent for Hamilton to nurse him in her abbey.

Thither was he taken, but he says that he lay speechless till Easter day. Now seeing that he spoke not French, the Abbess gave him to another to be nursed, to whom Hamilton told all his story just as it befell, and how Madame Saint Katherine had saved his life, and how he had made his vow to Madame Saint Katherine. Wherefore the Abbess loved Hamilton the better, and gave command that he should be more tenderly nursed. So it befell that the night between Easter day and Easter Monday there came a voice to the said Hamilton, saying to him, "Deliver thee, deliver thee! Bethink thee to accomplish thy vow in my chapel of Fierboys, and I will aid and guard thee."

Nevertheless it was fifteen days before the said Hamilton could walk or start, for his wounded foot harmed him more than ought else. Wherefore as soon as he could walk, he said farewell to the Abbess and set forth on his way to this chapel, and came here very slowly, for he could not walk by reason of his foot, which was not healed.

Then saith Hamilton that he found in the fields certain of his company, with whom he abode some days to get back his strength. But while he was there, on Saturday sennight, and was lying with certain of his fellows, but yet slept not, there came to him a voice saying :

"Already I bade thee and commanded thee to go and fulfil thy vow in my chapel at Fierboys, whereof thou makest no account. Wherefore acquit thee speedily of thy vow, and make no more tarrying."

Thereon the said voice gave him a great buffet and a sore on the cheek, and he says that those who lay with him awoke, and asked who had struck him. To which he answered them nothing, but so soon as day broke, he set forth on his way to come hither. And to-day the said Hamilton came hither in his shirt, bringing the halter wherewith he was hanged, and praised, thanked, and glorified the glorious Virgin, Madame Saint Katherine, for the grace which she had done him. And so hath he sworn on the Missal that all these things are true, in the presence of Messieurs Jacques Amissel, Jehan Bredar, priests; Brother Gilles Lecourt, Jehan Chermeteau, Jehan de Rameau, Guillaume Menost, and many others, over two hundred, who heard tell, and say, and proclaim the said miracle.

HE twenty-ninth day of March, in the year one thousand four hundred and twenty-nine, André Estourneau, an esquire of the parish of Manoc near Confoulant, hath said and declared the grace shewn to him by God, at the prayer of the glorious virgin, Madame Saint Katherine.

It is to be known that the said Estorneau left Rochefoucault on his way to Mareuil, on last Saint Valentine's day. And when he was near

Mareuil he met two Englishmen, his enemies, who took him and his page, and bound their feet straitly under the bellies of their horses, intending to bring them to the island of Madoc, or further. Then Estorneau was sore discomforted, and knew no remede, save only that he minded him of the fair miracles wrought by Our Lord at the prayer of Madame Saint Katherine of Fierboys. To her then he recommended himself right devoutly, that she would pray Our Lord to deliver him out of the hands of his enemies, so would he come to thank her in her chapel of Fierboys, in such guise as his enemies now held him.

Now after he had made his vow

and prayer, all his heart was lighter and more assured. And incontinent he had monition that he should escape. So took he the mantle on him, when now night was come, and rent it asunder, that he might fare the nimbler. And after they had gone a little way down a glen, approaching a river near Chales, the said pass being steep and perilous, there was he between the two Englishmen. So when he found himself in the steepest of that pass, he drew near him who rode foremost, and struck him such a blow with his fist between the shoulders that horse and man fell, and the horse dragged his rider. Then began the man to cry to his fellow, "Help, I perish!"

15

Thereon Estorneau crossed the path into a wood and so escaped. Then, having ridden half a league, he let himself fall backwards over the crupper of his horse, and undid his bonds, and so rode homewards at adventure, without way or path, all the night long. Yet never lost he his way, and many deep waters he forded, who had never been that way before.

Thus escaped Estorneau, by grace of God, and the prayer of the glorious Virgin, Madame Saint Katherine. And hath sworn that this is true, in presence of Messire Richard Kyrthrizian, Brother Gilles Lecourt, priests and warders of this Chapel, and Messire Jehan Bredur, priest, and others.

(A Latin Deposition.)

JEHAN BOUCHER, Licentiate in Law, Canon of Tours and Angers, and Dean of St. Jean in Angers, on Tuesday after Easter, that is, on the eighteenth day of April, in the year of our Lord one thousand four hundred and thirty, at my house in Angers, about nine o'clock at night, began to be sorely sick, with an intolerable headache that lasted till four o'clock in the morning, and, by reason of so great pain, I thought rather to die than to live. In that

hour I minded me of the glorious virgin Saint Katherine, to whom I was ever wont to pray on all occasions of need, and to her I recommended me, and made my vow. Then suddenly and instantly, by grace of God, and of that glorious Virgin, as I firmly believe, that intolerable pain ceased.

Within a few days, being well again, I set forth on foot to fulfil my vow and return thanks to God. In the chapel here I said Mass, both for the King, and the Maid, the worthy servant of God, and for the peace and prosperity of this realm, on Wednesday, May the fifth, in the year aforesaid.[1]

[1] The Maid was taken prisoner at Compiègne eighteen days after this Mass.

N the thirteenth of July, in the year one thousand four hundred and thirty, came on pilgrimage into the chapel Pierre du Fons of Bourges, who is of the company of Regnault Guillaume, brother of La Hire, and he set forth and declared the miracle wrought by God for him, at the prayer of Madame Saint Katherine. It is to be known that eight days before the feast of Saint Aignan the said Pierre and four of his fellows

were taken in a house or place named Lignières by the English of Alençon. Thence they were led to Alençon to prison. The first day of their coming thither the English cut off the head of one of the prisoners, for some displeasure that aforetime he had done them. And next day they hanged two more, so there remained only Pierre du Fons and one other. Now at the end of eight days their captain, Regnault Guillaume, sent to tell the English that such treatment as they gave his men, he would give theirs, which message the English held in high despite. So on the morrow they led Pierre and his companion forth of Alençon to hang them, who devoutly commended themselves to God and to Madame Saint Katherine. Now Pierre prayed the English to hang him last, that he might have time to implore the mercy and pardon of God. They therefore hanged his fellow first on a walnut tree, by the wall of Alençon, hard by a chapel of Madame Saint Katherine, whereby is a graveyard, and therein a ditch to bury the said prisoners, when once they were dead. Then Pierre again vowed himself devoutly to Madame Saint Katherine, praying her to beseech God for him, and the Virgin Mary, and to aid him, wherefor, if he could escape alive, he would come to thank and praise her in her chapel here. Then made they him to climb the said walnut tree and hanged him high from a branch thereof, where he remained hanging for half an hour, till they deemed him dead. Then they undid the halter, and Pierre fell on his feet on the earth, before all the company, there being present more than three hundred persons. Thereon they made him climb the said walnut tree again, and hanged him again, he that hanged him saying that he would fasten the knot so well that he might not undo it. There hung Pierre for more than half an hour, stirring neither hand nor foot, so that all deemed him dead indeed. So he who hanged him climbed the said walnut tree and cut the halter, that Pierre might fall and be buried in the fosse with his fellow. So fell he on ground, and straightway sat up and commended himself to Madame Saint Katherine.

Thereat were all who stood by sore astonished, that die he could not, and some said that he should not be hanged again, for that it was a God's miracle. Then two Englishmen took him and carried him up into the said walnut tree, and swore by the faith of their bodies that this time he should not escape. So they hanged him again, and one pulled at his legs as hard as might be, and the other pressed down with his feet on Pierre's shoulders, as heavily as might be, even till they deemed him dead and strangled. Then they climbed down and left him hanging for an hour and a half. Thereafter an Englishman climbed into the walnut tree and cut the halter, and Pierre fell to earth, who was carried to the said fosse, all deeming him dead. Then he sat up and opened his eyes, looking on such folk as were there, whereat all were amazed, and certain of the English said that this was manifest miracle of God, and that he should not be hanged more, or otherwise slain, for fear of God's anger. Therefore they bore him into the said chapel, and the captain of Alençon came to see him, and commanded that no evil or displeasure should be done him, but

122

that he should be given meat and drink.

There then abode he in that chapel for three weeks with two women to guard him, one French, the other English. But when the English woman saw that he began to get back his strength, she betook herself to murmur against him, and would have given him to an Englishman to be his prisoner. But the French woman told him this and bade find some remede, or they would send for him and make him prisoner. Thereon Pierre so wrought that he found means whereby Regnault Guillaume and his company heard that they should seek him in the said chapel, and they carried him away. Thus escaped Pierre du Fons out of the hand of his enemies by grace of God, and prayer of the glorious virgin, Madame Saint Katherine. All of this the said Pierre hath sworn to be true by the faith of his body, in presence of messire Richard Kyrthrizian, Brother Gilles Lecourt, warder of the chapel, Jehan Bredur, priest, Loys Forest, Robert Cornabel, and others.

N the twenty-third day of May, in the year one thousand four hundred and thirty-seven, came hither Marguerite de Mounay, a native of Normandy, and wife of a gentleman named Gilbert de Frenay, who also came hither with his wife. The said Marguerite had been prisoner in the town of Frenay le Vicomte, where she was held as pledge for her husband's ransom. Here lay she for five years and five months in irons, bound with an iron

chain, and fastened in a yoke, day and night, because her husband could not pay the great monies that were demanded of him.

She, then, as one out of all comfort, beholding that there was none who had pity on her, remembered her of the fair miracles daily done in the chapel in this place. So made she her vow to God, and the Virgin Mary, and to Madame Saint Katherine, that never would she drink wine till she had made pilgrimage to the said chapel, if by any means she might escape. And on the night after she had made her vow, namely on the twenty-sixth day of January past, there came to her a Voice, as she was falling asleep, which told her that she should be delivered out of prison. Thereon she again devoutly recommended herself to Madame Saint Katherine. Next day came the jailer, who let her go out of the yoke, that she might pass to the *chambres*. Then the said jailer went his way, and forgot to set her back in the yoke. Thereon Marguerite kneeled down, praying Saint Katherine to be her aid. Right so, when she had done her prayer, the irons and chains fell from her feet on one side, but not on the other. Then took she the said irons and chains, and hove them up to the height of her thigh, and fared to the door of the prison, that she found open, and so went forth down the street of

Frenay, about two hours before noon, in the sight of the English. Yet was there found no man to ask her what she did. Thus was Marguerite delivered, at the prayer of Madame Saint Katherine.

That all this is true she hath sworn; present, Messire Georges Guiot, curé of Saint Maur, and Brother Gilles Lecourt, warders of the chapel, Vincent des Patiz, Guillaume Guerrier, priests, and several others.

N the twenty-fifth day of July, in the year one thousand four hundred and thirty-seven, came into the chapel here one Thomas de Brique-ville, a knight's son, of the garrison of La Val, to whom God wrought fair grace at the prayer of the Virgin Mary, and of the glorious Madame Saint Katherine.

. It chanced that the said Thomas was for three years prisoner to the English in a castle named Saint Denis, and they asked for him a

ransom of a hundred *saluz*. He for
his part offered to pay sixty, which
the English would not take. Thomas
therefore made his vow to Madame
Saint Katherine, that, if she were
pleased to aid him, he would come
to her chapel in his shirt, barefooted,
and bareheaded.

Thereon he found a manner to be
rid of his irons, by help of two little
knives and a little hatchet, concerning which he hath never known
whence they came, save by grace
of God. Thus was he free from
bonds, one Friday at evening, and
so went forth on the wall. Anon
one asked him if he was about leap-
ing down, whereto he answered
" yea," and men ran after him, who

escaped to the foot of the wall, by grace of God and at the prayer of Madame Saint Katherine. Now the hour when he fled was sunset and moonrising. Thus has Thomas accomplished his vow, in the day and year above said, and hath sworn that his tale is true.

Present hereat the honorable and discreet brother Antoine de la Motte, Messire Georges Guiot, prior and curé of Saint Maure, Brother Gilles Lecourt, and others.

HE seventeenth day of the month of February, in the year one thousand four hundred and thirty-seven, came into the chapel here Jehan Moreau, of the parish of Ses in Normandy, who hath told and declared the grace wrought for him by God at the prayer of Madame Saint Katherine. It is to be known that, about four years ago, he was taken by the English in front of his own mill, and thence carried to Alençon with certain others, and there was put into a cellar, and set in irons

weighing twelve pounds, and at
night was in the yoke, and ever
hath been in this manner till the
month of August last. Then he and
three other prisoners in the said cellars remembered them of the fair
and manifest miracles which God
worked at the prayer of the glorious
virgin Madame Saint Katherine. So
made they their vows and commended them devoutly to her, imploring her to pray God that He
would be pleased to deliver them
from the prison, and the filth wherein
they were, and out of the hands of
their enemies.

Anon, their vow being made, they
devised a manner of escape, and bethought them of digging a mine in

the said cellar, but before they could devise no manner of remedy. So found they all how lightly they might undo their irons, and they mined till they won their way into a hall, whereof the doors and windows were barred and bolted, so that the prisoners knew not how to issue forth. Then marked they a window about the height of two men from the ground, and knew not how to attain unto it, nor by what manner of means they might climb thereto. So prayed they to Madame Saint Katherine, and then bethought them to put one of their irons into a hole in the said wall, whereby they climbed to the said window, and bent the iron, and turned the bolt, and crept through in their shirts. Then leaped they head foremost into the street, yet did themselves no manner of mischief, and in doing all this made great noise and uproar. Yet the jailer, who was lying above the said cellar, and all they of his company, some seven or eight men, all awake and devising with each other, heard nothing of the noise made by the prisoners. So passed they freely to the church of Our Lady in Alençon, and there were guarded by the English night and day for a month, save one of them, a Breton named Yvonnet le Camus, who was there but a week, and the English dragged him forth, for they held him in hatred.

Now the English ceased to watch the prisoners, deeming that they would not dare to leave the church. Which when the prisoners knew, they issued forth at seven o'clock in the morning, the hour when mass was said in the church; thence went they to the walls and ditches of the town, that were very deep, and harmed themselves not a whit, and lightly passed a great fence of thorns, and a row of pikes sharpened, then climbed the opposite bank of the fosse, which was a thing right marvelous. And the said Moreau declares that all those who have heard of this matter, and know the places through which they passed, are amazed at the adventure.

Thence they went to a chapel of Saint Blaise, about two arbalest shots from the town of Alençon. There they betook themselves in freedom, and were watched by seven Englishmen all the night following. But when it was day the English returned to Alençon, as not deeming that the prisoners would dare to escape in the day time. Then wandered forth the prisoners at adventure, commending themselves always to Madame Saint Katherine. So they left the said chapel about nine o'clock in the morning, and fared without hindrance, by grace of God and of Madame Saint Katherine. And to-day Moreau has betaken himself hither, all ironed on both legs, even as he promised when he made his vow. And he hath sworn by the faith of his body that all which he hath said is true, in presence of Messire Georges Guiot, Brother Gilles Lecourt, warders of the chapel, Jehan Chermeteau, Benoist Pinart, Gilles le Bouvier, Nicolas Mercier, Guillaume Pigeon, and several others.

HE thirteenth day of March, the year one thousand four hundred and thirty-eight, came into the chapel of Madame Saint Katherine of Fierboys, Jehan Moret, esquire, because of the fair grace which our Lord hath shown him, at the prayer of the glorious virgin, Madame Saint Katherine, namely, that Moret was taken and put in prison in a deep ditch, at the Castle of Angoulême. And there hath he lain for the space of fifty days and fifty nights.

Therefore he commended him to Madame Saint Katherine, imploring her to pray God for him, wherefore he would make pilgrimage to see her, if he might escape. Then anon he fell asleep, and when he woke found himself out of the ditch, and so escaped without ransom. And now is come to thank God here, and Our Lady, and Madame Saint Katherine.

EHAN DU RUS-LAY, dwelling at Saint Enthrope de Xaintes, declares that he was prisoner of the English at Conac, three leagues from Pons in Saintonge, and was held to ransom at thirty-five *reals*, whereof he had paid thirteen. And for that he had not paid the whole sum of thirty-five *reals*, the said English told him that they would carry him to Bordeaux and double his ransom. Then he being in great fear bethought him of Madame Saint Kath-

erine of Fierboys, and betook him to pray for deliverance from that pain wherein he lay. Then, anon, the prayer being done, and he lying in irons, the chains fell off his body, and the nail dropped out of its own accord. He therefore, so soon as he perceived himself free of his irons, took them and hid them under the straw. Then once more he prayed to Madame Saint Katherine that she would be pleased to convey him out of that place, and so took the road, and went forth to the gate of the castle, where were the porter and others playing at draughts. So went he forth out of that castle, and being forth met women coming from the wood, and pages that had been watering horses, but, by grace of God and of Madame Saint Katherine, no manner of mischief befell him; who hath come to-day within the chapel here to thank Our Lord, and the Virgin Mary, and Madame Saint Katherine, for the grace wrought for him by them.

That all this is true he hath sworn before Messire Georges Guiot, curé of Sainte Maure and warder of this chapel, Nicolas Mercier, priest, Jehan Lemaire, and others, this tenth day of March, in the year one thousand four hundred and thirty-nine.

IMON LOYS, of the parish of Saint Martin d'Orvillier, in the diocese of Amiens, came hither on pilgrimage, saying that, when he and certain of his fellowship were riding to succor the King of Hungary, they were taken by the Saracens, and were kept in irons as slaves, being chained by the legs and necks. Then bethought they of the noble miracles of Madame Saint Katherine. Anon, when they had made their vows, the chains and collars of iron on

their legs and necks fell off, and so escaped they without any hindrance. And the said Loys came to this chapel on the second day of October in the year one thousand four hundred forty and three, to thank God and Madame Saint Katherine. He saith also that it is now six months agone since he and his fellows commended them to the glorious virgin. And that all above said is true he hath sworn in presence of Messire Georges Guiot, priest, Brother Peter Queroan, warders of this chapel, Messire Jehan Quentin, priest, and divers others.

19

HE thirteenth day of the month of June, in the year one thousand four hundred forty and four came into this chapel one of the archers of Monseigneur the Dauphin named Jean Oquilhe, of the parish of St. Guidas of the Wood, in the see of Nantes, in Brittany. This man had been taken by the English and carried to la Rivière de Thibouville, and there put into stocks so great, heavy, and marvelous, that it needed four men to set him in and

take him out. He then, being in this prison, bethought him of Madame Saint Katherine, to whom he made his vow.

Anon, the vow being made, he issued forth of the irons and the prison, doing himself no manner of harm, and so crossed the ditches of the place, so full of water and so deep that it was marvel. Therefore the said Jean is come to do his vow and his pilgrimage. And hath said and sworn that these things are true, in presence of Messire Georges Guiot, priest, Brother Pierre Queroan, warders of this chapel, and several others.

HE Tuesday after the Fête Dieu, in the year one thousand four hundred forty and four, came hither Jehan Prevost, an esquire, to thank God and Madame Saint Katherine.

This man was struck by a culverin ball on the bone of the leg, and could find no cure nor no remedy, for the stone of the culverin abode fast in his leg. Anon he mounted his horse and made a vow to God, Our Lady, and Madame Saint Katherine. And he had not ridden a league, when the said stone came out by the same way that it went in, and fell to the ground. Thus by the grace of God and Madame Saint Katherine he was whole and well, as he hath said and affirmed to be true, in presence of Messire Georges Guiot, priest, Brother Pierre Queroan, warders of this chapel, Guillaume Guierrier, and several others.

N the thirteenth day of the month of July, in the year one thousand four hundred forty and six, Jehan Fary, a native of Scotland, minstrel of our Lord the King, came hither on pilgrimage, and said and swore that one of the servants of the King's garden was playing with a bow, and shooting a match with the King's archers. Now in shooting the said servant loosed an arrow which struck the said minstrel, and the arrow passed two fingers deep into

150

his head. He then, finding that he was wounded, recommended himself to Madame Saint Katherine, and now has come hither whole and well, and has brought with him the said arrow, and let fix it in a head of wax, weighing half a pound. And hath said and sworn that this is true in presence of Messire Guillaume Pigeon, Guillaume Galerneau, priests, Brother Jehan Dau, and Messire Georges Guiot, warder of the chapel, and several others.

www.ingramcontent.com/pod-product-compliance
Lightning Source LLC
Chambersburg PA
CBHW020235030726
47497CB00009B/3101